THE HEYDAY OF MIDLAND RED

Mike Greenwood and Malcolm Keeley

Ian Allan
PUBLISHING

First published 2005

ISBN 0 7110 3079 0

© Ian Allan Publishing 2005

Published by Ian Allan Publishing

an imprint of Ian Allan Publishing Ltd, Hersham, Surrey KT12 4RG.
Printed in England by Ian Allan Printing Ltd, Hersham, Surrey KT12 4RG.

Code: 0507/B1

Front cover: On a pleasant day in May 1964 we see 1951 Brush-bodied BMMO D5B 3856 departing from The Newarke bus station on Leicester local service L1. At this time Midland Red operated from four bus stations in Leicester: St Margaret's, Southgate Street (express services only) and Newarke Street, as well as The Newarke. The four bus stations were some distance from each other, keeping local enthusiasts pretty fit. No 3856 had been new in September 1951 and was originally allocated to Digbeth garage; in November 1963 it became an Eastern Division engineering float vehicle, having earlier spent some time at Hereford, Ludlow, Cradley Heath and Leicester (Sandacre Street) garages. It was quite a late survivor of the class, finally being withdrawn in March 1966. In the 1960s Midland Red was really struggling with staff recruitment and retention. The 'Vacancies' advertisements either side of the destination displays on double-deckers became a common sight during this period. *Martin Llewellyn / Omnicolour*

Back cover: Class CL3 touring coach 4239, comprising 1954 BMMO C3 chassis and 1962 Plaxton 36-seat coachwork, cruises through Pitlochry in August 1963, lucky Scottish heather in the grille. The replacement bodies were initially painted cream, but patrons were not impressed, so traditional red and black was soon applied. Cream bands remained until the next repaint; one suspects that this was the original cream retained to avoid having to deal with that curly signwriting. Just discernible through the nearside windows of the coach is the sign for MacDonald's Restaurant — clearly a traditional Scottish eating establishment rather than the fast-food enterprise that dominates the world today! *Peter G. Smith*

Title page: The black top applied to Midland Red coaches and buses with better seating for longer services was highly effective — a simple touch showing elegance and taste evidently beyond image-makers today. Twenty of the Leyland PSU3 Leopards with Willowbrook bodies bought in 1962/3 were so blessed. Here 5178 has escaped onto a Shrewsbury local service in September 1967. BMMO's equivalent model, the S17, is represented by 5683 alongside. *E. N. Pounder*

Left: Probably, but we'll do our best to remember and bring you back some memories! A cautionary transfer familiar for decades to exiting Midland Red passengers. *Mike Greenwood*

Introduction

The heyday of Midland Red? Hmm ……
interesting! Like some earlier authors in the
series, we have debated the disparity between the
probable true heyday and the availability of colour
pictures. One thing is certain: Midland Red's
heyday ended earlier than that of most bus
operators.

Midland Red (properly the Birmingham &
Midland Motor Omnibus Company Ltd, or
BMMO for short) had enjoyed the financial
backing of the British Electric Traction group
from the very beginning of its existence, being
registered in November 1904 and operating from
the next year. Nevertheless it was a battle for
predominance until the Road Traffic Act, 1930,
brought regulation and a measure of security.

The company's Chief Engineer, L. G.
Wyndham Shire, unable to persuade the
manufacturers of the early 1920s to produce large
buses with the nimbleness of the small ones run
by the 'opposition', decided to design and build
his own. Thus Midland Red redesigned the British
bus with its SOS (thought to stand for 'Superior
Omnibus Specification') Standard, beginning a
pursuit of engineering excellence that saw annual
updates despite small production numbers. Some
kind of heyday, surely, but few working under
Shire's martinet manner would have thought so.
There was no general manager during this period,
and in charge of the traffic side was the splendidly
named Orlando Cecil Power. He was evidently
much more human, but the company's growth,
like that of any other at a time of widespread
poverty and high unemployment, was being built
on low pay and fearsome discipline.

The years of World War 2 saw the end of the
Shire/Power era, and the company's management
structure was put on a more normal footing
(although not entirely — it retained a number of
peculiarities!) with the recently arrived

Chief Engineer, D. M. Sinclair, becoming General
Manager. A brilliant engineer, Sinclair had the
breadth of experience to ensure the traffic
department kept up to scratch too. He was not
enamoured by 'SOS' on the front of each of his
buses, ditching it in favour of BMMO, the initials
of the company's proper name. He shared,
however, his predecessors' preoccupation with
making more space for passengers, and his team
built wartime prototypes of single-deckers with
engines under the floor and entrances ahead of the
front axle. Bits of the concept were to be found on
prewar buses elsewhere, but Midland Red put the
right overall package together and had the
confidence never to build another front-engined
single-decker. Again, it had redesigned the British
single-decker, and it had several hundred
underfloor-engined vehicles on the road before the
big boys got their designs to the 1950 Commercial
Motor Show. Double-deckers remained front-
engined for the time being, due to the height
implications of underfloor engines, but
Midland Red completely modernised their
appearance.

Passenger demand expanded massively after the
war as people wanted to get out and about but
faced restrictions on car production, which was
largely reserved for export. The war had led to a
more relaxed social structure, epitomised by a
crusading if perhaps over-zealous socialist
government. The railway share in Midland Red
became state-owned, but BET remained private
and in control. A more relaxed spirit, lots of
passengers, new buses — surely a heyday?
Sinclair was shrewd enough to recognise that the
boom was a bubble caused by exceptional
circumstances. He needed more and more buses,
very little could be replaced, and a recurrent
theme in his column in the staff newspaper was
the importance of shifting all the passengers

Above: Now at the end of its life, adverts removed,
without the correct destination blinds and with
engineering 'float' status (*i.e.* not allocated to a
particular garage), 3819 exits Digbeth garage,
Birmingham, to take up service in 1966. These
premises were also Birmingham's coach station
(and still are, at the time of writing), hence the
Standerwick 'Gay Hostess' Leyland Atlantean coach
in the background. *Malcolm Keeley*

promptly and courteously to keep them travelling.

The year 1954 marked the half-century of
Midland Red and the formal opening of Central
Works, a rebuild of the old Carlyle Works that had
been underway ever since the end of World War 2.
This and new lightweight designs were keeping
the company prominent in the technical press,
despite the products' not being on general sale;
some S15-type buses were demonstrated to sister
BET companies, but, unfortunately, nothing came
of it.

On Whit Saturday 1955 a young enthusiast by the name of Christopher Davis cycled to the Malverns and, while there, decided to see what was working the twice-daily X91 Hereford–Leicester service. Powering up the long hills from Ledbury came S14 4257, the lightweight bodywork allowing the driver some extra 'oomph'. A new type of bus, gleaming — in itself a memorable sight. But the company was still enjoying its postwar travel boom, so following behind were two S13s, 3927 and 3918, and finally S9 3391 as quadruplicate, all no doubt flogging their fully laden way up in second gear, those early postwar engines threatening their characteristic chuffing as full revs approached. What a memory, what price a camera, what price sound video! This had to be the real heyday, surely. But evidence of decline was already becoming apparent; evening trade was disappearing as television became popular, and all sorts of rising costs (not least fuel tax) were damaging profitability. Rural services — a large part of the company's operations — were becoming increasingly a liability, although some drivers derived benefit from this, as the introduction of one-man buses brought an enhanced pay rate.

As the motorway age dawned, in 1959, Midland Red was ready with its iconic CM5T coaches. The latest D9 front-engined double-decker was attracting almost universal praise, soon followed by what was surely the high-spot of technical prowess in the form of the two D10 underfloor-engined double-deckers. In 1960 one could have believed that Midland Red was strong enough to last forever. Most of the fleet, apart from ageing double-deckers purchased to meet urgent fleet needs between 1948 and 1953 and a handful of secondhand buses recently acquired with Leicestershire independent operators, was designed and built by the company, while only the tiniest Midlands villages were not served by Midland Red or its Stratford Blue subsidiary. Midlanders enjoyed days out or top-quality tours all over the country in truly immaculate red-and-black coaches or sped along the new M1 motorway in a CM5T. At this time Midland Red carried around a million passengers each day on almost 2,000 vehicles and employed some 8,500 people through its varied activities.

The decline arrived suddenly and gathered pace as the '60s progressed. The increasing battering by rising costs coincided with the retirement of the old stalwarts. Whether in design, engineering or traffic, Midland Red could not replace them in sufficient numbers, due to the better conditions and higher wages being offered by the then thriving West Midlands car industry. Leyland and Daimler buses were purchased as BMMO's own production fell to an uneconomic rate (and ceased in 1970). The desperate staff shortages in all departments destroyed the reputation for reliability, and even proud tour coaches were pressed into service on bus routes.

The Labour government of the late 1960s aspired to complete the nationalisation of bus companies. BET was a shrewd organisation and, in its bus companies with large rural territories, had seen the future. It extracted the right price from the state, and ownership of its subsidiaries, including Midland Red, duly passed to the new National Bus Company. Meanwhile that same government had forced the West Midlands municipally owned bus undertakings to merge into the West Midlands Passenger Transport Executive, which was required to control all public transport in its area. In 1973 NBC sold Midland Red's West Midlands operations to

Left: Most of Stratford's bus services terminated alongside the Red Lion. The Leyland buses of Midland Red's Stratford Blue subsidiary were accompanied for many years by LD8-class all-Leyland PD2 Titans bought by Midland Red itself in 1952/3. Examples of Digbeth's sizeable allocation would appear on service 150 to Birmingham, but even more numerous were Leamington's, which turned up on a variety of routes. One of the latter, 4067, is seen in April 1965. *Malcolm Keeley*

Right: Two ready for the road at the entrance to Oldbury garage in August 1970. No 4772 (772 BHA) was the last D7 to be built (in 1957), while 4193 was a 1954 BMMO C3 rebodied by Plaxton in 1962, by now fitted with a roof-mounted destination box. *Malcolm Keeley*

WMPTE — a mistake it did not generally repeat elsewhere, settling instead for operating agreements with PTEs. But Midland Red lost its heartland and, with it, many talented staff. Curiously, despite the arrival of hard times, 1973 arguably marked Midland Red's geographical heyday, the company having finally absorbed its subsidiary, Stratford Blue, on the first day of 1971 and a cluster of independents just prior to the loss of some 413 buses to WMPTE in December 1973.

The sale to WMPTE was presumably to refinance the rest of Midland Red, but the remaining territory was too rural. In 1974 the company carried only a third of the number of passengers it had transported 20 years earlier but still employed more than half as many staff, despite the spread of one-person operation (OPO) and the fact that it no longer manufactured its own vehicles. Even after drastic surgery through network revisions, by 1981 NBC felt that the only

solution was to divide Midland Red into smaller companies. The Conservative government privatised these along with the rest of NBC, and they have changed hands more than once, their trading names altering as they passed to the new big groups.

Today very little trace of Midland Red remains except in preservation, notably at Wythall, where the Transport Museum splendidly keeps the spirit alive with a large collection of the company's buses and other artefacts and confirms the enduring interest in this iconic bus company. Anybody who remembers its heyday will have at least one indestructible memory like that of Christopher Davis and from time to time will travel to Wythall for another sip of classic 'Red' wine.

It is with a glance or two into the NBC corporate era that your authors have declared the end of the heyday of Midland Red. We hope you

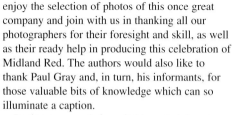

enjoy the selection of photos of this once great company and join with us in thanking all our photographers for their foresight and skill, as well as their ready help in producing this celebration of Midland Red. The authors would also like to thank Paul Gray and, in turn, his informants, for those valuable bits of knowledge which can so illuminate a caption.

During our search for suitable material we have endeavoured to use unpublished photographs and have managed to prise out a number of real gems stretching from the 1950s through to the 1970s. Undoubtedly there are still plenty of interesting photographs of this golden era out there. These are often in private collections, possibly taken by enthusiasts from outside the Midlands indulging themselves on trips to the Midland Red region. We are, of course, hopeful that this book will be sufficiently well received to encourage the publishers to consider another volume sometime in the future. Accordingly we would urge anyone who took photographs of Midland Red, especially in colour, before 1970 to contact us via the publishers.

Mike Greenwood
Malcolm Keeley
January 2005

Left: Extremely long services like the 112-mile X91 were part of the appeal of Midland Red, as described in the accompanying text. The X91 was operated with dual-purpose single-deckers by the garages at each end, Hereford and Leicester Southgate Street; the buses would meet at Stratford-upon-Avon, where the crews would swap over to return to their 'home' end. At times of pressure Southgate Street would call upon garages like Hinckley and Nuneaton for duplicates. The duplicate would show the ultimate destination even if that particular vehicle was terminating short, requiring the passengers to be transferred. This is a rare example of a double-decker duplicate — in this case D9 5010, provided by Leicester Southgate Street garage — seen at Pool Meadow, Coventry, on Spring Bank Holiday Monday (27 May) 1974. The D9 was most unlikely to travel beyond Stratford, on account of the low bridge between Evesham and Worcester.
Mike Greenwood

Left: The territorial decline could be said to have started here. The Walsall Road group of services was a big operation for Midland Red, with four garages contributing. The Urban District of Perry Barr had been added to the City of Birmingham in 1928, but, by agreement, Midland Red continued to operate the routes until the workings entirely within the city were transferred to Birmingham City Transport in 1957/8. The first to change operator were the Beeches Estate services on 1 September 1957. Here at the terminus in Hassop Road, with a BCT 'Bundy' time-recording clock already half installed, are BMMO D7s 4496 and 4402, the latter on a short working as far as Six Ways, Aston. No 4496 eventually became a towing vehicle (see page 73) and lives on, preserved at the Transport Museum, Wythall. *Chris Banks*

Above: By great good fortune a 1939 SOS FEDD also presented itself for the photographer. No 2335 (FHA 839) is about to turn right off Walsall Road into Beeches Estate to conclude an evidently unremunerative evening-peak journey. This design of forward-entrance double-decker had been the standard model since 1934, and 2335 belonged to the last batch. These later deliveries had Brush bodywork, which required extensive rebuilding *c*1950/1, the flush-mounted glazing with top-sliders being the most obvious change. *Chris Banks*

Left: Midland Red's S6 design, with its underfloor engine and front entrance, is historically of immense importance as the trend-setter for single-deckers throughout the country. The batch of 100 vehicles, delivered in late 1946 and during 1947, represented the fruition of wartime development work. They started a new fleet-number series, 3000-99, with the bodywork contract being divided equally between Brush and Metro-Cammell. Detail differences — rain-strip, headlight positioning and around the rear end — were discernible to the skilled eye. No 3018, a Coalville garage Brush-bodied example, is being readied for its return journey to Ashby-de-la-Zouch from Leicester's St Margaret's bus station. Like all the early postwar single-deckers, 3018 was lengthened from its original 27ft 6in to 29ft 3in, enabling the seating capacity to be increased from 40 to 44. The work on the entire S6 class was undertaken by Roe in 1953. *Mike Sutcliffe collection*

Below left: Buses to the newly permitted width of 8ft arrived in 1948, appropriately designated the S8 class, the modified windscreen design being the easiest way of identifying the wider vehicles. Minor design changes produced the similar-looking S9 and S10 classes, while the last to this style were the S12s, constructed in 1950/1 to the new length, to which the earlier buses were subsequently rebuilt. Long-lived S8 No 3268 is seen at Newport, Shropshire, on a Sunday working in June 1965.
Malcolm Keeley

Right: Determining the precise location in Leicester of this shot of BMMO D5 3482 certainly proved something of a challenge! Although the church, the 12th-century St Mary de Castro, still exists the other landmarks have long since gone, and the surrounding area has been significantly redeveloped. However, we are pretty sure that the shot was taken in Southgate Street, as the bus made its way from the Midland Red garage to take up service at The Newarke in the winter of 1964. The BMMO D5 was an 8ft-wide postwar production version of the D1 prototype. The D5 class was made up of 100 vehicles, all with 56-seat Brush bodywork, delivered in 1949/50. No 3482 was one of a number allocated to Leicester's Southgate Street garage in the summer of 1949 to replace the ageing SOS REDDs. Many were to remain as 'one garage' buses, including 3482, which was eventually withdrawn in August 1964. *Mike Sutcliffe collection*

Left: Everybody else's 1949 coaches were front-engined half-cab jobs, soon rendered obsolete by underfloor-engined vehicles. Midland Red was ahead of the pack with its C1 class of 45 coaches, and they still looked modern enough to be acceptable until the mid-1960s. Duple built the bodies to BMMO design. CM5Ts may have been running up and down the motorways for years, and National white coaches might be only nine years away, but 3321 is clearly representative of an earlier, more genteel coaching era at Taunton in July 1963, its white-coated driver absolutely in keeping. *John Carroll*

Above: As with all large operators, the regular turnover of road staff necessitated a sizeable driving school. At the time of their withdrawal, in the mid-1960s, many of the C1s were still in very good condition, and nine of the batch were accordingly retained for driver-training duties. A number were converted to dual-control, incorporating a nearside steering wheel. They included 3341, a long survivor in the training fleet, lasting until 1976. The coach is seen at rest at Coventry's Pool Meadow bus station on Spring Bank Holiday Monday (27 May) 1974; no bank-holiday rest for the instructors or recruits, such was the need to keep on top of the staff-recruitment requirement. Behind 3341 can be seen D7 4397, another member of Nuneaton garage's driver-training fleet. *Mike Greenwood*

11

Above: The 12-strong C2 class, delivered in 1950, were outwardly similar to their C1 brethren but were intended primarily for extended tours and seated only 26. As new coaches arrived in the mid-1950s the batch were gradually re-seated to a capacity of 30. No 3349 was still looking immaculate when photographed on 23 August 1964. Such was the popularity of the nearside front seats that the two venerable ladies clearly are not prepared to risk losing their prime position at the obligatory refreshment stop. *Derek Bailey*

Right: Midland Red could not build enough buses for its own needs immediately after World War 2. Not surprisingly, it concentrated on producing its advanced designs of underfloor-engined single-deckers, not receiving any of its D5 double-deckers until 1949. The requirement for double-deckers was answered by 100 AEC Regent IIs (the AD2 class), with bodies fully to BMMO design, and 20 Guy Arab IIIs. The Guys, which were classified GD6 by Midland Red, were delivered in 1949 and had Guy bodies on Park Royal frames. They had powerful 10.35-litre Meadows 6DC engines and, allocated to Dudley garage, made short work of the town's hills until 8-litre BMMO engines were substituted in 1952! This is Guy 3575. *Chris Aston*

Above: One of the 1950 BMMO S10 models, 3703, was fitted with independent front suspension and designated S11 until conventional suspension was fitted in 1957, around the time of this shot in Walsall Road, Perry Barr. With all the double-deckers in use on the Walsall Road group of services, it is perverse that the bus through to Walsall is a saloon on this occasion. However, risk of overcrowding by short-distance riders was reduced by the imposition of a minimum fare on peak-period journeys, the advisory notice being clearly visible on the windscreen. *Chris Banks*

Right: The 100 BMMO D5B buses of 1950-2 were the first Midland Reds built with enclosed platforms and power doors and were used initially on longer services requiring double-deckers. They were rather heavy, and later types would offer a better power:weight ratio. However, with their comfortably appointed bodies built by Brush, the D5Bs proved very sound buses on local services, 3800 being shown passing the front of its home garage, Stourbridge, in August 1963. *Mike Greenwood collection*

Left: The bulk of the S13 class were delivered in 1952/3, with 40-seat dual-purpose bodywork by Brush or Nudd Bros & Lockyer. During 1956 they were repainted into the then current coach livery of red with black roof, to which was added a polished aluminium strip around the waistline, giving these buses a certain elegance. In this view, recorded at St Margaret's bus station, Leicester, in May 1964, 3950 demonstrates the lack of a partition behind the driver, the most memorable feature of riding on an S13. *Chris Aston*

Right: When, in the early 1950s, requirements once more outstripped BMMO production, it was again the double-deck fleet that received buses of outside manufacture, 100 Leyland PD2 Titans with Leyland's own bodywork, modified to Midland Red's ideas on concealed radiators, being delivered in 1952/3. These constituted the LD8 class, and at one time no fewer than 35 of them were based at Birmingham's Digbeth garage. No 4013 had recently received the benefit of a spray repaint at Central Works when seen at Knowle. Prior to its October 1956 arrival at Digbeth it had been on hire to Stratford Blue for several months, being quite at home amongst the Leylands there. Leamington's 4046 was similarly loaned for several weeks in the winter of 1959/60. *G. H. Stone*

Left: Midland Red drivers relied entirely on hand signals until the end of the 1950s; flashers were not legalised until the middle of the decade, and the company's buses did not have the benefit of semaphore trafficators either. An exception was LD8 4009, seen at Worcester, which received experimental flashers. Although later 1950s buses subsequently had these fitted retrospectively, 4009 would remain the only LD8 so blessed. *Martin Llewellyn / Omnicolour*

Above: Some idea of the importance of the Walsall Road, Birmingham, services can be gauged from this shot at the Scott Arms, on the Birmingham boundary and terminus of short workings, not long before handover of the latter to Birmingham City Transport in 1958. Bearwood's D7 4161 has unloaded and is turning to join the D7 and LD8 ready to return to the city centre. Although splendidly appointed and maintained, the replacing BCT buses would lack the platform doors and heaters of these buses! *Chris Banks*

19

Left: The Dudley Road trams out of Birmingham were replaced in 1939 jointly by Birmingham City Transport Leylands and, from Oldbury garage, the last batch of Midland Red SOS FEDDs. BMMO D7s eventually took on the Midland Red responsibilities and had a very long innings, as the operators did not agree to larger-capacity buses until the PTE era. Seen in June 1968, 4108 was an early (1954) D7. By this time road alterations obliged the B87 and companion routes to turn left out of Edmund Street after years of turning right into Congreve Street. *Malcolm Keeley*

Above: No fewer than 350 D7s were built between 1953 and 1957, Metro-Cammell building the lightweight bodies to BMMO design. No 4531 passes Jephson Gardens, Leamington Spa, while serving a virile destination in 1971; S17 No 5574 follows. The D7 was another subsequently converted as a recovery vehicle, being one of two that passed to WMPTE. *Mike Greenwood collection*

Above: Seen enjoying a relatively relaxed existence at Shrewsbury in December 1970, 4114, despite being one of the first D7s, would go on to become the last in service, finally succumbing in March 1973. Its last five months, however, would be under a much tougher regime, at Dudley; a few months more and it would have joined the WMPTE fleet. This particular D7 had a deeper windscreen. *John Carroll*

Right: A few D7s passed through works late enough to receive the final style of lettering to be applied before the introduction of National Bus Company corporate livery. Digbeth's 4732 circumnavigates the large Robin Hood island in Hall Green, Birmingham, in watery March sunshine in 1972. *Malcolm Keeley*

Left: Apart from Leylands acquired from absorbed operators, D7s were the last manual-gearbox double-deckers in the fleet. Some had extended lives, cut down as recovery vehicles, whilst others remained complete as driver-tuition buses. Here a potential driver gingerly steers 4130 from New Street into Stephenson Place, in the very heart of Birmingham, during September 1973. *Malcolm Keeley*

Right: Some 75 coaches were built in 1953/4, of which 63, with Willowbrook 37-seat bodywork to Midland Red design, constituted the C3 class, the remaining 12 being C4-class 32-seat touring coaches whose Alexander bodywork looked almost identical apart from the inclusion of curved glass panels in the roof coves. Seen *c*1964, awaiting passengers at the coach stand in Humberstone Gate, Leicester, C3 No 4209 was a long-term resident at the city's Southgate Street garage. The C3 alongside has its passenger door open, revealing the style of moquette upholstery. *Peter G. Smith*

A typical scene repeated day in, year out, across the Midland Red network, as a BMMO single-decker waits unobtrusively for passengers. In this case the date is *c*1964, the location Nuneaton bus station, and the bus one of the S14 class, 4668, new in November 1957. The S14 was designed at the height of the company's obsession with minimising weight, its structure being so light that single rear wheels were possible, albeit at the expense of ride quality. *Peter G. Smith*

Right: A splendidly evocative shot of two S14s — 4259 and 4293 — very early in life, working 'day tour' duties. The date is 2 April 1956, the location Burford, in the Cotswolds. Despite the buses' being numerically quite close, there are a number of detailed front-end differences between them.
Brian Knowlman

Right: The S14 had a dual-purpose (bus/coach) equivalent, the S15, which had better seats and finish and more usual double rear wheels. Like their S13 predecessors, the S15s were eventually allocated to more mundane work and lost their black tops. Eleven-year-old 4637 awaits its next duty at Bearwood bus station in 1968. *E. N. Pounder*

Left: The 219 S14s at first glance all looked identical but, like other types in this highly innovative fleet, the class bristled with experimental items, either actively on trial or long since rejected but still fitted. Shrewsbury's 4700 has hopper side ventilators of a style not adopted by Midland Red. *Mike Greenwood collection*

Above: What should have been the 220th S14 was instead the 1958 prototype of a new coach, the C5. In styling terms 4722 moved well away from the curvy lines of its predecessors, and its 'lantern' windscreen would become the most recognisable feature of the company's iconic motorway version, the CM5T, introduced on the first day of the M1 in November 1959. No 4722 enjoyed a more ordinary existence as an express coach, differing from the 64 production examples principally at the rear end. From 1967 the 'black top' livery was briefly replaced by maroon on repaints, as apparent from this view recorded at the junction of Stratford Road and School Road in Hall Green, Birmingham, in October 1969. *Malcolm Keeley*

Left: BMMO C5MT motorway coach 4804 in its prime at Birmingham's Digbeth Coach Station, with proud driver, awestruck small boy and very respectable passengers, including an Audrey Hepburn lookalike in green hat. *Transport Museum, Wythall, collection*

Above: What happened to those CM5T motorway coaches when displaced by 36ft-long CM6Ts in 1965/6? No 4815 lost its turbocharger and toilet and became a C5A service bus at Hereford garage. Its glamorous London career a distant memory, it roams the highways of Shropshire in August 1969. *Ted Jones*

Left: Over the years Midland Red purchased numerous small independent operators to fill gaps in its system and to eliminate competition. The desire was always the acquisition of the relevant road-service licences, and such vehicles as existed were never taken into stock. Well …… almost never. In May 1930 eight ex-Great Western Railway buses passed into the Midland Red fleet with the transfer of the GWR's Black Country services, and in 1936 six of the more modern members of the acquired Leicester & District Bus Co fleet were operated. However, a curious situation occurred when the long-established Leicester independent Kemp & Shaw was acquired, on 31 July 1955, the business being operated as a subsidiary, and the fleet of seven Guys and two Leylands continuing to run in Kemp & Shaw livery. Here EJF 669, one of a pair of 1948 Northern Counties-bodied Guy Arab IIIs, stands inside the Sandacre Street, Leicester, garage in 1957. Note the distinctive garage notice, which created a challenge to the dedicated Midland Red bus spotter. *Mike Sutcliffe collection*

Above right: The last bus purchased by Kemp & Shaw, in 1952, was JBC 989, an all-Leyland PD2/12. Numbered 31, it is seen here at Leicester's St Margaret's bus station shortly after acquisition in 1955. The bus had already received an 'SA' (Leicester Sandacre Street garage) destination blind and would have its entire front destination display converted to standard Midland Red pattern soon after. In the background is another of the Kemp & Shaw Guy Arabs, whilst behind the PD2 is a Midland Red FEDD. *Mike Sutcliffe collection*

Right: On 1 January 1959, when Kemp & Shaw was finally liquidated, eight of the Kemp & Shaw buses passed into the main BMMO fleet, taking fleet numbers 4838-45. The second of the all-Leyland PD2s, 4844, a lowbridge PD2/1 of 1950, leaves St Margaret's bus station on 6 July 1965. Kemp & Shaw had purchased this lowbridge bus to enable it to maintain a double-decker service from Leicester to Derby after severe storms had washed away the road bridge at Shardlow, the replacement Bailey bridge being able to accommodate a double-decker of only lowbridge proportions. Also in this photograph is 4051, one of Midland Red's own Leyland-bodied Leylands. Nine members of the LD8 class spent some of the latter part of their lives at the Leicester-area garages. *Mike Sutcliffe collection*

Left: The acquisition of Kemp & Shaw also brought two Barnard-bodied Guy Arab III single-deckers. No 4843 is photographed at the rear of Wigston garage in August 1963. Next to the Guy is 3188, a Metro-Cammell-bodied member of the AD2 class. *Mike Sutcliffe collection*

Above: As already stated, the retention by BMMO of vehicles acquired with businesses was a very rare event. However, shortly after the total absorption of the Kemp & Shaw fleet, further second-hand vehicles were added, upon the takeover of another Leicestershire company. The acquisition of H. Boyer & Son, Rothley,

on 1 February 1959 added to the fleet two Sentinels and one Leyland which were repainted into Midland Red livery and numbered 4846-8. No 4848 was typical of early underfloor-engined Leylands, being a 1952 Royal Tiger with Leyland's own 44-seat bodywork. The photographer, a noted Leyland fan, had to wait a fair time before the opportunity came to get this shot 'in the can'. The location is St Margaret's bus station in Leicester, with 4848 waiting for its next duty whilst Hylton & Dawson's 1952 Leyland coach-bodied Royal Tiger, RPG 807, waits to make another trip to Glenfield on 27 September 1965. *Mike Sutcliffe collection*

Left: The last major acquisition of an operator in Leicestershire was that of L. D. Brown ('Brown's Blue'), in March 1963. On this occasion the large fleet, of more than 50 buses and coaches, was not absorbed, although the rather dilapidated garage at Markfield was acquired. The last Brown's Blue working was the 10.25pm Coalville–Ibstock service on 15 March 1963. Fortunately photographers were on hand to record the occasion, and here we see ex-London Transport RT164 (HLW 151) awaiting departure time in Marlborough Square, Coalville. The Brown's Blue fleet at takeover contained 14 second-hand double-deckers, including many RTs. Midland Red transferred a number of S14s and D7s to the Markfield garage to take over the services. Three D9s and an S17 were also allocated new to Markfield before the garage was closed in 1968 and the displaced

buses and workings transferred to the nearby Coalville garage. *Mike Sutcliffe collection*

Above: The BMMO D9 took advantage of the newly permitted length of 30ft for double-deckers. Early drawings show D7 styling modified in fairly frightening ways, but the actual prototype, which took to the roads in 1958, showed nearly all the promise of the design classic to follow — one of the most handsome half-cab double-deckers ever produced. The big (10.5-litre) new engine, coupled to a semi-automatic gearbox, meant drivers liked them too. No 4773 waits for time at Coleshill terminus late in its career. The bus was withdrawn in 1972 but fortunately has been saved for preservation. *Mike Sutcliffe collection*

Above: The first of the 344 production D9s entered service in 1960/1. The first batch, comprising 94 buses, included 4903, photographed in Nuneaton bus station. After its Midland Red career was over, this was one of seven D9s purchased by Obsolete Fleet to launch open-top sightseeing services in London.
Mike Greenwood collection

Right: Dudley's buses not only had to contend with the tough terrain; the height of the town centre means it is very exposed, especially to cold weather from the east. Two D9s challenge arctic conditions in January 1968; just about to turn from Priory Street into Wolverhampton Street, 5348 leads the bus honoured with the fleet number 5000. *Paul Roberts*

Left: Two first-batch D9s circumnavigate Victoria Square, Birmingham, in June 1972. They shared a similar history, but their futures would be very different: 4910 would continue working from Tamworth for the rest of its Midland Red life, but 4863 would find itself absorbed into West Midlands PTE 18 months later. From 1966 the company went through a confused period in terms of lettering and transfers, employing several different styles, sometimes dependent on the type and age of bus. It finally settled on this rather attractive style, but all would be swept away by NBC corporate livery, introduced later in 1972. *Malcolm Keeley*

Above: BMMO D9s 4941 and 4945 had a reduced number of side ventilators, but these were of the hopper type, and some were later replaced by the usual sliders. No 4945 enters Colmore Row, Birmingham, in June 1973 — the wheels are already NBC corporate grey, but the rest of the bus remains traditional. A D9 on a Chelmsley Wood service was relatively rare; the construction of the large estate coincided with the introduction of one-person-operated double-deck buses, so the local population became used to paying on entry from the outset. *Malcolm Keeley*

Above: Midland Red further surrendered its presence on the Walsall Road out of Birmingham when the 118 became jointly operated with Walsall Corporation. The latter was absorbed into West Midlands PTE from 1 October 1969, and, of course, Midland Red's services such as the 118 followed in December 1973. Shots of Midland Red buses on these services alongside buses in WMPTE livery nowadays look a bit odd, as the situation pertained for only a short time. Here, in March 1972, D9 No 4995, of Bearwood garage, prepares to enter St Paul's bus station, Walsall. The ex-West Bromwich CVG6-30 is one of 27 Daimlers transferred to Walsall following conversion of the 74/79 group of services to one-person operation; interestingly it is 248H, the example preserved at the Transport Museum, Wythall. *Malcolm Keeley*

Right: The CM5T motorway coach was an extremely rare example of a provincial bus produced as a diecast model, enhancing the charisma of Midland Red to the 1960s generation of enthusiasts. In recent years we have been blessed with a huge range of diecasts. The Original Omnibus Company has not only reproduced the C5 and derivatives but has also produced an excellent small-scale representation of the D9. One version is 5413, advertising a dog track. Here is the real thing in Pershore Street, Birmingham, in June 1973. *Malcolm Keeley*

Left: In the late 1950s Midland Red was impressed by the high capacity of double-deckers being produced by other manufacturers but did not wish to participate in the then fashionable (and unreliable) rear-engined concept. The D9, considered by many to be of revolutionary design, was quickly eclipsed by the unveiling, in 1960, of the first BMMO D10 prototype. The new vehicle was a high-capacity, underfloor-engined, 30ft-long chassisless double-decker. No 4943 was a 78-seater and entered service in January 1961. The second prototype, 4944, which followed in April 1961, was a 65-seat version with a second staircase on the offside rear and a narrow exit doorway and platform behind the rear axle. The twin-staircase experiment was not successful, and in November 1962 No 4944 was rebuilt to single-staircase format. Both D10s were sent to Leicester for a short period, 4944 being seen at the city's Southgate Street coach station, waiting to operate a journey on the X68 express service to Birmingham. The date is 6 February 1964. *Mike Sutcliffe collection*

Above: Sadly, for various reasons — the changing fortunes of the company, the need for further development and, possibly, influence from outside — it was decided not to put the D10 into production. The two prototypes settled down to busy but uneventful careers working from Stafford garage. In August 1971 4943 was photographed at Dudley bus station. The family resemblance with the D9 is readily apparent when comparisons are made with 5044 parked behind. By 1973 both D10s had been withdrawn from service, but fortunately 4943 was secured for preservation, and this revolutionary bus is now part of the large Midland Red collection at the Transport Museum, Wythall. *Ted Jones*

Left: The rebodying with Plaxton Panorama 36-seat coachwork of some BMMO C3 coaches (newly designated CL3) for the 1963 season produced an extraordinary combination but avoided the need to evolve a new but inevitably small build of touring-coach design. Even more controversial was the cream livery originally applied, soon replaced by traditional red with black and then (from 1967) maroon relief, as seen on 4239 at Shrewsbury in October 1969. From November 1970 the maroon relief would itself give way to all-red. The diamond-shaped Midland Red sign on the office (right) is unusual. *Ted Jones*

Above: Some of the Scottish coach cruises could not cope with vehicles longer than 27ft 6in, so three of the 1950 BMMO C2 touring coaches were also rebodied, receiving Plaxton Embassy 26-seat coachwork and being redesignated CL2. The shortage of maintenance staff by July 1970 meant that 3350 was being knocked around on ordinary bus services intended for 63-seat double-deckers instead of being carefully groomed for its next Scottish cruise. The former traffic flyover at Camp Hill, once familiar to south Brummies, provides the backdrop. *Malcolm Keeley*

47

Left: Detail alterations to livery and polished trim on the second batch further improved the appearance of the S15. Attractive though the red-and-black combination was, the restriction of the darker colour to the roof brightened the appearance considerably. In September 1965 No 5088 waits in Southgate Street coach station, Leicester, ready to operate the X69 to Coventry. Note that the bus has been driven through the bus wash, a regular procedure for express buses exiting the adjacent Southgate Street bus garage to take up service; also the scotch (usually a magnificent casting) placed forward of the nearside rear wheel, another common

Midland Red practice. Sadly we shall never know the title of the book in which the waiting passenger is so engrossed! *Mike Sutcliffe collection*

Above: All-over red demoted S15 5085, in Paradise Street, Birmingham, during May 1971 has been working the Birmingham–Dudley–Wolverhampton service and is now on its last trip, terminating at Dudley, its home garage. The conductor has not wound off the 'via' blind, making the overall presentation look rather silly. *Malcolm Keeley*

49

Left: In 1962 Midland Red introduced a 52-seat version of the S14, to be built to the new maximum dimensions of 36ft long by 8ft 2½in wide permitted for coaches and single-deck buses. Designated S16, it was not entirely successful, mainly because it was underpowered, and it was unpopular with drivers because it retained an unfashionable manual gearbox. Worcester-based 5115 loads at the town's bus station ready for the trip to the Malverns. As well as carrying the later-style livery 5115 has new upper- and lower-case destination blinds, which became the vogue in the early 1970s. Its final days would be spent on loan to City of Oxford Motor Services. *Mike Greenwood collection*

Above right: With performance and ease of operation in mind, Midland Red introduced the BMMO S17 in 1963. Outwardly identical to the S16, the new type was fitted with a 10.5-litre BMMO engine coupled to a semi-automatic gearbox. Rather surprisingly another batch of S16s entered service in 1964, principally to use up stocks of manual gearboxes and 8-litre BMMO KL engines. Second-batch S16 5522 is seen late in its career at North Gate, Aldridge, operating an ex-Harper Bros (of Heath Hayes) service. The Leighswood Circular was a peak-hour-only operation, known by drivers as the 'Whizzer', on account of the ease with which they could complete the circuit in about half the allocated running time. Harper Bros had been acquired by Midland Red in 1974. *Paul Roberts*

Right: The arrival of the S16s and S17s allowed for the mass withdrawal of the early-postwar single-deckers. In 1963 three S9s, 3372/4/85, were cut down as tree-cutters, the result being workmanlike yet still attractive. Here we see former bus 3385 being used for its intended purpose, in this case clearing the way for service 281 in The Broadway, Dudley. By the time the shot was taken, in 1970, a rather flat gold underlined fleetname was being introduced to the fleet. *Paul Roberts*

Above: In order to supplement its own vehicle production Midland Red purchased 100 Leyland Leopard PSU3/4 single-deckers in 1962/3. Although to BMMO requirements, the bodywork was to the BET Federation style. LS18-class Leyland Leopard/Weymann 5155 waits for departure time at Nuneaton bus station. The bundles in the front window are probably newspapers to be dropped off *en route*. Midland Red was very willing to carry parcels, from the very early days right up to the 1970s. Tariffs were published in the company's timetables but noted that 'Bicycles, perambulators, large push chairs, wet fish, or other unsuitable packages, cannot be accepted for conveyance on buses at any time'.

Right: The body order for the LS18 class was split between Weymann and Willowbrook. Weymann bodied the first 25 vehicles, and of the balance Willowbrook finished 20 as dual-purpose 48-seaters, which were delivered in the attractive red-and-black livery. All the LS18 buses were finished as 53-seaters. By now fitted out for one-person operation, Willowbrook-bodied 5203 was photographed in ex-works condition in Memorial Square, Coalville, on 23 April 1972. The small white sticker seen here on the driver's side window proclaimed that the vehicle was not to be mechanically washed until a defined date. *Derek Bailey*

Above: Midland Red also supplemented the double-deck production line, with the purchase of the DD11 class. Daimler supplied the Fleetline chassis, and these were bodied by Alexander in Falkirk. Certainly disproving the legend that Midland Red built all its own buses, 5272 from Birmingham's Digbeth garage precedes Leamington's LD8 Leyland 4046 up Trinity Street, Coventry, *c*1964. The 50 DD11 buses of 1963 were not the first rear-engined buses in the fleet, the company having dabbled with the concept in the late 1930s. *Mike Greenwood collection*

Right: DD11 5282 was delivered new to Leicester Southgate Street garage in 1963 and was still giving good service to the city's populace when photographed in Humberstone Gate in the early 1970s. The highly profitable Scraptoft–New Parks service was actually the L29, but a poorly wound number blind gives a completely different impression. Note the conductor on the platform, double-deck one-person operation still being in its infancy. *Mike Greenwood collection*

Above: Think of the features that represent the best of Britain, and Bridgnorth probably has them. Fine views, a glorious river, a cliff railway, splendid buildings, a broad selection of eating places and, of course, a superb steam railway. Sadly, as everywhere else, there are no longer genuine Midland Red buses serving the hinterland. Kidderminster S17 5620 loads in the High Town in May 1973. *Malcolm Keeley*

Right: Mention has been made earlier of Dudley's arctic tendencies. Here the attempt by S17 5727 to take the short route into the bus park has met with calamity. The reversing light is on, and a host of staff are attempting to push it back onto the main highway. Meanwhile a snowballer is sizing up his next target! We are truly thankful that the photographer braved the elements in January 1968 to capture this remarkable scene, not forgetting the crews, of course. One suspects they were not saying how pretty the snow looked! *Paul Roberts*

Left: The prototype of a larger motorway coach, the CM6T, was unveiled in 1963 and was visually very much like a lengthened CM5T, even including route boards. The original CM5T lantern-style windscreen was soon modified to the style depicted here, which it carried for the rest of its service life. It was stored from September 1972, being officially withdrawn the following March; this photograph was taken on 8 July 1973. *Derek Bailey*

Above: Some 29 production CM6s followed the prototype in 1965/6. Most were CM6T models, with toilets, but 5667-71 were built without the feature, for the Birmingham–Worcester express services. No 5674 was the last to be built and entered service in a Labour-run world where private enterprise in the bus industry was soon feeling under threat. This August 1967 view at London's Victoria Coach Station shows it wearing anti-nationalisation notices, but three months later British Electric Traction announced that it was selling all its British bus interests, including Midland Red, to the state. Twenty years later the Conservatives privatised it all, and New Labour has been content to leave it that way. Some of these contrary political decisions must be wrong! *John Carroll*

Left: One of the BMMO CM6 class, 5667, works an express service to Birmingham on 25 June 1972. The coaches were extremely comfortable and somewhat potent, especially when 'opened up' on the motorway. They were very dependable workhorses, and many enthusiasts can recount interesting tales that earned the class something of a cult status. *Derek Bailey*

Above: BMMO CM6T 5654 appeared in May 1971 rebuilt as a CM6A type with some bus fittings. A year later it returned to coach work and, in due course, received NBC white coach livery. This shot, however, shows it in Edgbaston Street, Birmingham, on long-distance bus route X99 to Nottingham in April 1974. The CM6 coaches had short lives, being withdrawn between 1972 and 1974. *Malcolm Keeley*

Above: Fifty Leyland coaches joined the fleet in 1965. Nos 5774-5822 were Leopard PSU3/4R chassis with 49-seat Duple (Northern) Commander bodies, designated LC7. In September 1965 5787 of Wigston garage waits on the coach stand in Humberstone Gate, Leicester, the prospect of an Evening Tour on board the new coach having thus far failed to attract many punters. The 50th Leyland coach was a shorter Leopard L2T model; numbered 5823, the sole LC8 carried a 36-seat Plaxton Panorama body for use on extended coach tours. *Mike Sutcliffe collection*

Right: A further 15 Leopards entered service in 1966. Classified LC9, these coaches were the shorter PSU4/4R model and carried Plaxton Panorama I bodywork. Originally used on extended coach tours, 5838 was still performing this role when photographed on 24 July 1971. Bound for Scotland, the well-turned-out coach waits for more customers at Lichfield bus station. *Derek Bailey*

Left: There were only 10 vehicles in the dual-purpose LS20 class. These 1967 Leyland Leopards with long-window Willowbrook bodies looked striking when new, the red supplemented by subtle brightwork and the classic black roof. No 5840 was surrounded by coaches from further afield when photographed at Pool Meadow, Coventry, in April 1968. *Malcolm Keeley*

Above: The loss of the black relief and disinterest in masking trim upon successive resprays made the LS20s increasingly look down at heel. When photographed in April 1972 Digbeth's 5839 was about to commence a journey from Acocks Green on the long-established short suburban service to Sheldon. None of the later dual-purpose Leyland Leopards would pass to WMPTE, as they were intended for the longer bus services, which remained with Midland Red, and the luxury coachwork of 5839 would become just a comfortable memory on routes such as this. *Malcolm Keeley*

Left: The final BMMO production run consisted of 143 vehicles (5849-5991), originally intended to be further S17 models, which took from 1967 to 1970 to enter service as production slowed down. In the event there were three different grades of accommodation (30 semi-coach S21, 37 dual-purpose S22 and 76 bus S23) in a modified body with longer windows and, at last, the emergency exit transferred from the rear wall to the rear offside. The first S21s arrived early enough to be given black roofs, but, in common with all such vehicles from 5860 onwards, 5871 of Swadlincote garage entered service with maroon roof. Birmingham's famous Rotunda building is behind the photographer; today 5871 would be in the middle of a pedestrianised area facing the malls of the latest incarnation of the Bull Ring Shopping Centre.
Malcolm Keeley

Below left: Representing the S23 class is 5937, photographed along the Parade, Leamington Spa. It was built in 1969 and was one of the last to be completed at Carlyle Works. That final accolade went to 5941, which, after a small ceremony at Carlyle Works, entered service in January 1970. The remaining 50 buses (5942-91) were completed at the Plaxton coachworks in Scarborough.
Mike Greenwood collection

Right: The S22s were all-over red from new and looked rather bland for luxury-seated vehicles, but the grille may have suited more people's taste than the flashy salesman's grin of the S21. In August 1973, Bearwood's 5911 slips into St Paul's bus station, Walsall, between WMPTE Daimler Fleetlines from Walsall and West Bromwich corporations. In contrast with its retention of the newer Leyland Leopards, Midland Red was content to pass luxury-seated BMMO vehicles to WMPTE, and 5911 changed hands four months later. *Malcolm Keeley*

Left: Brand-new DD12 5998 parked opposite Leamington's Old Warwick Road garage. When Midland Red took the decision to stop producing its own double-deckers it was the Alexander-bodied Daimler Fleetline that was ordered in quantity. Clearly satisfied with the performance of the DD11s delivered in 1963, the company took a total of 149 broadly similar DD12s, delivered in 1966-8. The 1966 batch introduced a new fleetname style and also had very small fleet numbers; they were also notable in being the last Midland Red double-deckers delivered with moquette seats on both decks, subsequent vehicles featuring PVC. The notice at the entrance to the railway station is interesting; presumably, by inference, no such restriction applied to the Stratford Blue or G&G buses that also used the forecourt! *Mike Sutcliffe collection*

Above: 'Sixties psychedelia spread to buses, and it has to be said that some of the early all-over advertisements were works of art, even if they look a touch over-energetic today. DD12 5999 searches for its unloading spot in Colmore Row, Birmingham, in May 1973. *Malcolm Keeley*

Left: An at-a-glance guide to identifying DD11 and DD12 models is offered by Leamington-based Fleetlines 5267 and 6128 at Pool Meadow, Coventry, on the first day of August 1973. The most obvious recognition point became unreliable when many DD11s lost their upper-deck front ventilators. Here we have a livery contrast too, as 5267 has already gained NBC poppy red. *Malcolm Keeley*

Above right: Built in the late 1960s, the huge Birmingham overspill estate of Chelmsley Wood was located outside the city boundary, and it thus fell to Midland Red to provide the bus services — something it was not too happy to do, bearing in mind the shortages being suffered in all departments. The company's management, unlike its drivers, became rather more enthusiastic about dual-door Daimler Fleetlines, purchasing more than 100 to form its DD13 class after this 1966 DD12 was modified from single-door. No 6023 looks lost amid the estate construction in 1968. *E. N. Pounder*

Right: DD13s 6156-6225 of 1969 looked like DD12s with an extra door, but for the last batch of 33 (6261-93), delivered in 1970/1, Alexander applied subtle changes to the body styling. Not only had BMMO production ceased; these also represented the last quantity delivery of double-deckers to Midland Red; 10 years later, when the company was split, areas like Leicester would be desperate for big buses. No 6279 of Bearwood garage rounds the island at the Holly Bush on Hagley Road West, Birmingham, in March 1972. *Ted Jones*

Left: The first single-deck buses to be ordered following the closure of the BMMO production line were a batch of 100 45-seat Plaxton Derwent-bodied Ford R192s. Delivered to the company in 1970/1, these were classified S25 (the outside manufacturers' prefix letter having now been dropped) and represented a low-point to some enthusiasts of the company! No 6323 is seen at the rear of Banbury bus station when new. The lurid green Formica visible through the windscreen also featured on the seat backs, the story going that the colour was the result of research conducted to find what colour was least likely to induce motion sickness. It also featured on some Leopard deliveries. *Paul Roberts*

Below left: The 100 Ford/Plaxtons polished off the remaining 1950s S14s and S15s. Manual-gearbox and frugal, they were most suited to rural services. Sadly these country routes were struggling; No 6297 of Shrewsbury garage is an empty bus in an empty landscape at Bayston Hill in June 1971. *Ted Jones*

Right: Despite an original intended life of just seven years, many of the Fords gave long and reliable service. So it would be ungallant to suggest a link between the Fords' arrival and the conversion of no fewer than 11 D7s to towing lorries between 1972 and 1974. Nevertheless, this one would appear to be attending to Ford 6391 at Evesham! The D7 is our old friend 4496 (see page 6), still around today at the Transport Museum, Wythall. *Paul Roberts*

Left: Had Midland Red imposed its own products on its Stratford Blue subsidiary then this would have been a BMMO D5 — there's a mental picture to conjure with! Stratford Blue was finally absorbed on the first day of 1971, by which time all the seriously handsome all-Leyland PD2 Titans had gone. No 26 of 1950 poses for the tourists in the yard next to the garage in the centre of Stratford. *Mike Sutcliffe collection*

Above: The last day of Stratford Blue, with a line of Northern Counties-bodied Leylands at the exit of the Stratford garage. No 27 was a 1963 Titan PD3/4; whilst 133 and 135 also had 1963 bodies, these were mounted on 1950 Leyland PS2 Tiger chassis, their original half-cab single-deck bodies having been rendered obsolete before the chassis were worn out. All three had started life with different numbers — Stratford Blue seemed to have a problem with numbering, of both fleet and routes! When the fleet was absorbed Midland Red added 2000 to the fleet numbers. *Richard Butler*

Above: Once a proud member of the Stratford Blue coach fleet, 436 GAC had already been demoted to stage-carriage work prior to the Midland Red takeover. A 1963 Leyland Leopard PSU3 with Duple Alpine Continental coachwork, it became 2055 in the Midland Red fleet and when repainted red received the dual-purpose silver fleetname style. It passed to City of Oxford Motor Services in 1973. *Mike Greenwood collection*

Right: Most of the ex-Stratford Blue fleet was soon sold, but the last new vehicle to enter service, this one-off 1970 Alexander-bodied Leyland Leopard, had a longer life and travelled widely about the Midland Red network. This classic shot taken in January 1982, with frost still gripping the trees at lunchtime, shows 2036 near Craven Arms, Shropshire. By this time the company had been split and 2036 was part of the Midland Red (North) fleet, lasting until the end of the year, working from Ludlow garage. Happily the bus is now preserved in original Stratford Blue condition. *Ted Jones*

Left: Midland Red's coach fleet was still considered top-notch in the early 1970s, and the excursion programme well-patronised and highly regarded. The 1971/2 coach fleet intake consisted of 15 C12-class Plaxton Panorama Elite II-bodied Leyland Leopard PSU4B/4s. No 6456 basks in the Continental sunshine on 26 August 1972 whilst on a tour to Austria and the Black Forest. By this date Midland Red's classic coach livery was being replaced by NBC white — an imposed scheme repeating the marketing error Midland Red made 10 years previously with the cream-painted Plaxton rebodies. *Derek Bailey*

Above right: In 1971 Midland Red received a batch of 52 dual-purpose Leyland Leopard PSU3A/2 buses with 49-seat Willowbrook bodies. Designated S24, they were numbered 6394-6445. Photographed at Victoria Coach Station while on hire to United Counties, 6427 has a good load of passengers waiting for departure to Nottingham on 1 July 1972. The route number should be MX1, but for its own services Midland Red required letters on only the first track of the number blinds. *Derek Bailey*

Right: Thirteen more Leyland Leopards, this time with Marshall 53-seat bus bodywork, were delivered in 1972. Allocated fleet numbers 6461-73, the class was designated S26, the odd quantity (not for the superstitious!) believed to arise from the fact that three were intended originally for Stratford Blue. This batch ended the fleet-numbering series adopted on vehicles from March 1944, the next batch of new vehicles, 58 Leyland Nationals, starting a new series commencing at 101. S26 No 6465, a Swadlincote bus, was photographed in Wetmore Park bus station, Burton-upon-Trent. *Paul Roberts*

The NBC years. No more BMMO buses, no more double-deckers, no more Midland Red livery. Nevertheless, a repaint could still present a brave sight, as demonstrated by BMMO S17 No 5628 outside Malvern garage in July 1976. This was one of Midland Red's most attractive garages, opened in September 1954 and displaying many of the architectural features favoured by the company's in-house design staff. Sadly the need for economy led to the garage's closure only three months later; the S17 passed with the work to Worcester garage and was itself withdrawn the following year. The heyday had passed! *Chris Banks*